FAVOR
WITHOUT LIMITS

IT'S NOT JUST AN OPPORTUNITY, IT'S AN EXPERIENCE!

Lisa Fambro
MINISTRIES

LISA FAMBRO

WESTBOW
PRESS®
A DIVISION OF THOMAS NELSON
& ZONDERVAN

WestBow Press books may be ordered through booksellers or by contacting:

WestBow Press
A Division of Thomas Nelson & Zondervan
1663 Liberty Drive
Bloomington, IN 47403
www.westbowpress.com
1 (866) 928-1240

Because of the dynamic nature of the Internet, any web addresses or links contained in this book may have changed since publication and may no longer be valid. The views expressed in this work are solely those of the author and do not necessarily reflect the views of the publisher, and the publisher hereby disclaims any responsibility for them.

Any people depicted in stock imagery provided by Thinkstock are models, and such images are being used for illustrative purposes only. Certain stock imagery © Thinkstock.

Unless otherwise noted, scripture taken from the New King James Version®. Copyright © 1982 by Thomas Nelson. Used by permission. All rights reserved.

Scripture quotations marked (NIV) are taken from the Holy Bible, New International Version®, NIV®. Copyright © 1973, 1978, 1984, 2011 by Biblica, Inc.™ Used by permission of Zondervan. All rights reserved worldwide. www.zondervan.com The "NIV" and "New International Version" are trademarks registered in the United States Patent and Trademark Office by Biblica, Inc.™

Scripture quotations marked (AMP) are taken from the Amplified Bible, Copyright © 1954, 1958, 1962, 1964, 1965, 1987 by The Lockman Foundation. Used by permission.

Scripture taken from the King James Version of the Bible.

Scripture quotations taken from the New American Standard Bible® (NASB), Copyright © 1960, 1962, 1963, 1968, 1971, 1972, 1973, 1975, 1977, 1995 by The Lockman Foundation Used by permission. www.Lockman.org

Scripture quotations marked (TLB) are taken from The Living Bible copyright © 1971. Used by permission of Tyndale House Publishers, Inc., Carol Stream, Illinois 60188. All rights reserved.

ISBN: 978-1-5127-8688-0 (sc)
ISBN: 978-1-5127-8689-7 (hc)
ISBN: 978-1-5127-8687-3 (e)

Library of Congress Control Number: 2017907880

Print information available on the last page.

WestBow Press rev. date: 08/22/2019

To my parents, Brenda Best-Royal and (in loving memory) Ulysses Royal Jr., who made my life possible through the Lord Jesus Christ. You made me the "Best-Royal priesthood" a woman could ever grow to be! No one could have taught me better to expect God's best and never settle for less than what I've been destined for. Thank you for constant prayer and encouragement. I am blessed and highly favored to have been raised by you!

To my siblings, Rhonda, Shelly, Rhachel, and Ulysses III, I love you dearly!

Acknowlegments

First and foremost, I would like to give thanks to my Lord and Savior, Jesus Christ, for gift of the Holy Spirit. I thank God for revelation and trusting me to impart these words into the lives of people everywhere.

To my husband, James, thank you for always speaking life into me and pushing me to a level of greatness no other person could ever push me to! For all your sacrifices, unwavering love, and support, I am truly blessed! Thank you for continually covering me in prayer. I can truly say you favor me.

To my sons, Elias, Joel, and David, thank you for giving me a better understanding of what favor really looks like! Believing God for conception and and receiving my miracles shifted my faith to a whole new level. I know all things are possible for those who believe.

To my Royal family and my Fambro-Goldsmith family,

thank you for your support. God knew what he was doing when he connected me with you! Our family is truly blessed.

To Christian Growth Center Church and all of those who have spoken into my spirit, thank you for believing in me.

Introduction

Favor is God's advantage in your life. *Charitoo* (Greek) means "to endow with" and "to cause to find favor." the greek word also means, "freely bestowed."

John 15:16 says, "You did not choose Me, but I chose you and appointed you to go bear fruit." The first thing we need to know is that God chose us. He is the one who picked us out. Favor has been on your life since the beginning of time. When your father's seed met your mother's egg, it beat out all other components, just to form you. He chose you. Jeremiah 1:4 states, "Before I formed thee in your mother's womb, I knew you and called you into the nations." God strategically ordained your genetic makeup, DNA, blood type, height, and stature. He favored you into existence. Favor also comes from the Greek word *ratsah*, which means, "to be pleased with." So the second you entered life, God Himself saw you and spoke *ratsah* all over you. Your hair and skin color have been specifically chosen to bring pleasure to God. God truly feels pleased with you.

Psalm 41:11 states, "By this I know that you are well pleased with me." God's favor is for life, and we, as a chosen body of Christ, can experience this God kind of favor every day of our lives. Leviticus 26:9 says, "for I will look upon you with favor and make you fruitful and increase your numbers, and I will keep My covenant with you." From the day of your birth until the end of your life, God has made an agreement, and He will confirm the freely bestowed blessings He has commanded for you. Favor is available all day, every day. God releases this favor so that the will and purpose and plan of God can be done in your life. When your destiny meets up with sovereignty, favor can be released on your behalf. It can't be earned, but because God chose us, we are granted His unmerited favor.

I have a definite purpose for releasing this book. I believe that many are experiencing God's favor all day, every day, but don't even realize it. In this era, favor has become a sort of popular saying, phrase, or decree. Favor is not limited to fine cars, good jobs, position, or titles. Real favor, true favor, is so much more than that. In Biblical times, the favor of God was demonstrated in several ways. It is my desire to enlighten

His people on how you can experience godly favor. You are as entitled to the unmerited favor of God as those who have received it before you, from the beginning of time. As you read through these chapters, I believe God will reveal how you might not be rich, popular, or known by many, but that you are living in His unmerited favor. Pay close attention as you witness the many manifestations of the favor of God.

Contents

1

The Visitation

 "Rejoice highly favored one, the Lord is with you. Blessed are you among women, but when she saw him." She was troubled at his saying in and considered what manner of greeting this was then the angel said to her, "Do not be afraid, Mary, for you have found favor with God."

—Luke 1:28–30

Mary had the privilege to bring forth the greatest seed of all times. She was picked out and chosen to give birth to the Son of God. This is the same favor spoken about in Leviticus 26. God looked upon Mary, made her fruitful, and established His covenant with her for generations to come. *Favor should be agreeably reverenced and consciously walked in.* For some believers, it is hard to receive God's divine favor. Could you imagine how hard it could have been for Mary to believe that God had chosen her for this specific task? When the angels set out to the city, Mary was on God's mind! She was about to experience *charitoo* (meaning she was about to be found favorable) in God's eyes. All Mary had to do was receive it according to the Word of the Lord. Mary stated, "Be it done

3

unto me according to thy word." The word of the Lord is so powerful; as a believer all you have to do is receive it.

To receive means to take something that is offered, sent, or paid for; it means to accept or acquire and, in this case, it means to experience and be a recipient of God's great favor. His Word declares in Psalm 102, "You will arise and have compassion on Zion, for it is time to show favor to her; the appointed time has come." God has decided to bless you, so get ready to receive it!

To experience favor for life is to know the nature of God, the love of God, and the will of God. Guilt and condemnation are often the two biggest factors that rob believers of their God-given right to walk in favor. Guilt keeps you locked into your past and will cause you not to receive the mercy of God and realize His forgiveness. The Word declares, "Cast your sins into the sea of forgetfulness and He will remember them no more." Do not let past failures or present fears keep you from receiving the favor of God. Mary had a mandate, a high calling, and a God-given purpose. She was to bring forth the Savior to the world. Mary had to receive God's favor for life. This free gift required Mary to open her heart and spirit to the blessing from God.

The Supernatural

Mary is described as a virgin (*parthenos*). This refers to a person who is unmarried and has had no sexual relations with another person. Luke describes Mary's pregnancy as supernatural—of or relating to phenomena beyond or outside of the natural that are attributed to a deity, a divinity, or the Divine. Luke 1:35 states, "The Holy Spirit would come, the power of the most high would overshadow her and she would conceive." The following three experiences would occur.

1. Favor
2. Supernatural
3. Manifestation

God's favor is *supernatural*. It cannot be explained by a human being or determined by natural laws. It's a phenomenon that can't be figured out. What Mary believed but did not understand, we should believe, as well. Luke 1:37 states, "No promise is impossible with God."

Psalm 30:5 states, "For His anger is but for a moment, but His favor is for a lifetime and in His favor is life." Just as it was spoken to Mary, I say, rejoice this day for God has granted you His favor. Expect the supernatural to bring about a wonderful manifestation in your life.

Have you ever felt as if it could have only been God who showed up, intervened, or performed a miracle? Have you ever experienced something that could only have been the supernatural? Many times we have experienced visitations from angels or the blessing of a divine word, not realizing it's one of God's ways of showing favor.

I can remember when I became a new believer. Within the first six months of salvation, I was working in a small strip mall in Atlanta, Georgia. A certain individual appeared hovering over me, a gentleman, who was very tall and casually dressed. When he spoke to me, it was as if he were staring right through me. He asked the question, "Are you saved?" I replied yes. He, in turn, very sternly stated, "You represent Jesus everywhere you go!" Well, it was as if every word came out in slow motion. He suddenly turned around and walked away. I watched him walk to the middle of the mall; he was looking straight ahead without addressing one person. At the time, I knew he had come specifically for me. I knew he was an angel. Glory to God! He began to come back my way, headed forward, and then disappeared right before my eyes. I began to weep under the presence of God. I called my future husband, who was my fiancé at the time, and screamed, "I just had a visitation from an angel!"

The words the angel had spoken to me changed my life forever. To be humble before God when His message appears to us is a sign of receiving His unmerited favor. God uses spiritual means at times to relay natural messages, Hebrews 1:13–14 states, "But to which of the angels said he at any time; are they not all ministering spirits sent forth to minister for them, and who shall be heirs of salvation?"

Any time we have an experience like this, we should recognize that a visitation from an angel is God's divine favor. The Bible records many of these instances, as exemplified earlier with Mary. Another example can be found in Genesis 18:2–3. "Abraham lifted up his eyes, and three men stood by him as he ran to meet them." He declared, just on the basis of the visitation, that he had found favor in the Lord sight. *Never take for granted a divine occurrence when you know, beyond the shadow of doubt, that the event or message was sent from God.* It's not hard to experience the favor of God, but it can be difficult to recognize where and when it is being released in our lives.

2

The Covenant

And the Lord said, I will destroy man whom I have created, both man and beast, for it grieves Me and makes Me regret for I have made them. But, Noah found favor in the eyes of the Lord.

—Genesis 6:7–8 AB

We all know the story of Noah and the ark, including the two times two and the rain and the flood. When I first read the beginning, it amazed me see that God considered Noah and his family with favor (*charitoo*). Why did He? Genesis 6:9 states, "For he was a just and righteous man, and he walked in habitual Fellowship with God" (AB). Two characteristics that caused Noah to find favor were righteousness and continual fellowship. ea encapsulated by the Greek word *charitor*, which means the "freely bestowed blessing." It is not God who separates Himself from us, but our sin that will separate us from God. Freely bestowed blessings cannot be manifested where there is sin and evil at work. *Sin will cut off the manifestation of God's favor.* The Bible states, Genesis 6:9 "Noah was a just man and perfect in his generations" (KJV). Now, in a sense, *perfect* is a word that often intimidates believers and scares away unbelievers. But in other translations of the Scripture, Noah was *upright* or *righteous* in the eyes of God. *Perfect* comes from the Greek word *tamin*, which describes Noah's entire relationship with God; it means he met all the requirements of God's law. To be upright simply means "morally correct" or "to follow a law or standard." Noah was considered righteous, in right standing or right relations with God. The Hebrew word for *righteous* is transliterated as *zaddak*, meaning one who pursues the right course. Noah was not involved or knowingly engaged in sinful acts. His intentions were pure, and his imagination was not continually evil (Genesis 6:5).

As a believer, can say your intentions are pure and that you seek to follow the laws of God and conduct yourself with morally high standards? Then you are one who has found favor in the eyes of God. The Word declares, "Noah walked with God"; Genesis 6:9 the Amplified Bible says that Noah "walked in and had mutual Fellowship" with God. Noah had a relationship with God; there was constant communication between them. They shared frequent fellowship and communion, and Noah repeatedly worshipped God. Naturally, the more time you spend with someone, the more you know his or her mindset, nature, and even characteristics. This is what trnsspired between God and Noah; continual fellowship brought about an eternal relationship between them. Noah had a covenant!

Genesis 6:18 states, "But I will establish My covenant [promise, pledge] with you and thou shall come into the ark, thou and thy sons, and your wife and your sons' wives with you." When God establishes His favor with you, His favor spreads to your family, your seed, and your seed's seed. The Word states that God's blessings last for a thousand generations. It is for you and all the generations of your family to come. Even as you're reading this book, you can receive God's favor and decree it for your seed and your seed's seed in the name of Jesus! Say this now: "I receive the favor of God!" The same covenant promise and pledge that was given to Noah and his family is available for my family, as well as for yours. I do walk upright. If you do, too, you are just, and by His blood you are made righteous. I receive God's grace and His divine favor for my life. As God has remembered Noah, He also remembers you.

If you are a believer, you have a blood covenant with God. It is through this blood that you are made righteous. Now all you have to do is receive from the Lord. Psalm 5:12 states, "For thou, Lord will bless the righteous with favor. You will surround him, as with a shield." As long as you are in right standing with God, not only does His blood cover you, but His favor also surrounds you. When the Scriptures speak of the flood and the sparing of Noah and his family's life, there is no indication that Noah questioned God, felt unworthy, or asked "why me?" But continually, it reads "thus did Noah" and "Noah did according to all God commanded."

It wasn't hard for Noah to realize God spared his life, because he had been in constant fellowship with the Lord. Some say that favor is undeserved access, but Proverbs 16:15 says, "In the light of the Kings countenance is Life and His favor is as a cloud of latter rain." Time with God will produce the manifestations of the shield that surrounds you. Fellowship releases you to greater blessings than you have today. Look for His favor to manifest on your behalf through your obedience. God will produce a wellspring (or favor) of His latter rain.

Favor with Purpose

With favor comes great responsibility. It is not just a gift to be taken without any intention on giving back. As seen in the two prior chapters, Mary had great responsibility to be used as the vessel to produce, nurture, and take care of our Savior in earthly form. Having received this gift of favor, do you think Mary or even Joseph, who was her covering, could have abused our Lord, who in turn was their son? And Noah, for instance, had a major responsibility to be the only father on earth to begin humankind all over again. Noah was a watchman for his sons, their wives, his wife, the animals, and the land. What a position that the favor of the Lord imposed upon him! Favor is given to all who will receive it, walk upright, and practice habitual fellowship with God. But it is also given with great responsibility. It is God's pleasure to release one of His greatest gifts, but you must know that it comes with purpose.

3

Favor and Purpose

The Lord was with him; he showed him kindness and granted him favor in the eyes of the prison warden. So the warden put Joseph in charge of all those held in the prison, and he was made responsible for all that was done there.

—Genesis 39:21

There is a purpose to God's favor in your life. Joseph is a prime example that God's favor flows from the beginning of time until the end. Joseph, at the age of seventeen, was favored by his father Jacob over all his brothers. Genesis 37:4 states, "And when his brother saw that their father loved him more than all his brethren, they hated him, and could not speak peaceably to him." When the favor comes, so does the opposition that often results in hostility or antagonism. It may appear that this opposition is against you, when it actually is against your purpose and the destiny or plan you were created for. Joseph had a clear vision concerning the dream God gave him. When telling his brothers, he wasn't asking their opinion of his dream; instead, he wanted their undivided attention. He may not have known exactly what the future would manifest for him, but in his spirit, he knew there was a gift from God ahead of him. Because of his dream, his brothers envied him and were jealous of his sayings. Favor from God and other human beings will always produce enemies. But if God is for you, who can be against you? The hostility from Joseph's brothers pushed Joseph directly into his purpose. It doesn't matter what appears to come against you; if you can see your dream, God will give you favor to accomplish it. Open your mouth, and declare what saith the Lord. The enemy is very intimidating, and the one thing he wants to do is stop your vision, your dreams, and your faith-filled words.

Scriptures state that without vision, God's people perish; they are without substance, purpose, or destiny. They cease to live. Favor, however, brings destiny and purpose. To seize it, you must see it. See doors opening! See positions being created for you! See the coats of many colors being placed upon you! Genesis 29:2 says, "But the Lord was with Joseph, and though he was a *slave*, he was a successful and prosperous man in the house of his master the Egyptian" (AB).

Even when it appears that you are bound or at the bottom of the totem pole, favor will bring great success. There was a reason Joseph was a slave in Potiphar's house. As stated earlier, favor comes with great responsibility. Genesis 39:5 says, "And it came to pass from the time that he had made him overseer in his house, and over all he had, that the Lord blessed the Egyptian's house for Joseph's sake." Favor is what manifested for Joseph. No matter where he was placed, he found favor, and all that he did flourished. As a slave, he prospered. In the prison, he was given great responsibility and was shown mercy and loving-kindness. Joseph was being prepared for his purpose. When favor is in your life and there is a dream inside of you, God will connect you with the right people to help bring the dream to pass and to help the manifestation of God's favor to flow without ceasing. Favor was always in Joseph's life. However, Joseph was not afraid to speak about what he saw, which released him into the purpose that he was created for. While the Enemy may try to distort your vision through natural circumstances, make it clear that favor will release you into your destiny. Always say it! Say it! Say it! Say what God says in His word. Proverbs 18:22 states, "Life and death are in the power of the tongue." Some may say it's what Joseph said that sent him to the pit, but it's actually what he said that caused the favor to flow. In mere humility, he said what he saw in the spiritrealm. The Enemy wants us to be intimidated by the ways in which God has blessed us. Speaking these things isn't prideful or arrogant but a sign of our confidence that only God can bring your destiny to pass. You can have what you say! Open your mouth and say what God says! This process shows you are in agreement with His will for your life. Romans 4:17 says Call those things that be not as though they were. Words have power, confessing God's word brings possession. Whether you feel that you're living in God's favor or not. Confessing these things will produce a manifestation of what you say. Perhaps you feel as if you've been thrown into the pit or have served time in prison, but this feeling is working for your good. The beginning of labor is often hard to understand. God's ways are not our ways, and His thoughts are not our thoughts. What you might be experiencing now, in troubled times, does not dictate what your future will look like.

God is willing to raise you up, give you a testimony, and reveal His purpose for your life. Never stop decreeing what saith the Lord! There's a palace after the pit and prosperity after famine. Genesis 45:8 states, "So now it was not you that sent me, hither, but God; and He has made me a father to Pharaoh and Lord to all his house and a ruler throughout the land." It may seem as though you are in a pit, but if you will receive the favor of God for your life, the pit is only a stepping-stone to the next level, which is the palace! And I am here to tell you that not even your enemies can stop you— not circumstances, sickness, disease, abandonment, poverty, or prison. Instead, your enemies shall be your footstools. As He did for Joseph, God will prepare a table before you in the presence of enemies. Favor will keep you free when it appears that you should be bound. That is why the same condition or circumstance that you went through will be what consumes your enemies. That is called the "manifestation of favor" or "God's unmerited favor," which is His grace. No matter how much you messed up, the Lord continues to bless you. His anger lasts but a moment, but His favor is for life.

4

Favor with an Assignment

According to the American Heritage College Thesaurus, the word *assign* means to appoint and send to a particular place. It also means to set aside or apart for a specified purpose. To select for an office or position. Assign can also mean to elect, name, or nominate.

Favor often comes with the assignment; that is, it often comes with a name or position. To say "God has favored you" is to say "He elected you for a specific task." He nominated you, even when it didn't appear that you were qualified for the job. Favor will give you a name; it will raise you up, set you in the position, and give you the King's heart. Proverbs 16:15 states, "When the King smiles, there is Life; His favor refreshes like gentle rain."

One Door

And Esther obtained favor in the sight of all them that looked upon her.

—Esther 2:15

There is somebody somewhere reading this book whom God is preparing for greatness. Have you been wondering what's going on in your life? If so, this is a prophetic word from the Lord for you. This is not just a book or chapter; nor is it some words on a piece of paper. It is a prophetic word.

Job said, "If we decree a thing it shall also be established," so I decree the Esther blessing of all who read and receive this word in the name of Jesus. Remember that the Esther blessing is not just for women but, as the Bible says Esther 10:2 "the account of greatness" of Mordecai, who went from being outside the gate to being advanced into the king's court and placed second in command to the King. Are you ready for the Esther blessing? It is the decree of *favor*!

Everybody wants favor, and many are talking about it, praying about it, and seeking favor out. But I must tell you that favor is looking for you. There is a time and a season for favor to be manifested in your life, and you don't want to miss it! Favor makes an appeal. It sends out a request and says, "Who do I want to fall on this time? Who do I want to fall on this season?" There are certain seasons during which the hand of God extends. When there is a shift in the natural, there is often a shift in the spiritual. Don't you miss it!

However, let me advise you that there is a place you have to be in your life for the favor to flow freely. Because favor is not just for you; just like the anointing, it's released to bring glory back to God. We must always remember that to whom much is given, much is required. If your flesh is not crucified, you won't be able to handle the gift of favor. Favor testifies of the King, the omnipotent One, the omnipresent One, the El Shaddai, the God who is more than enough! It brings glory back to God, the almighty One!

The Bible tells us, "Then said the king's servants that ministered unto him, let there be fair young virgins summoned for the king" (Esther 2:2). In order to be included in the number when the request came for a new queen, a woman would have to be a fair young virgin. So if you weren't a virgin, you couldn't be considered for the position of the queen. Many of us want certain positions, and we believe God for the manifestation of His favor, but we have yet to display the qualities to step into that particular place. Before I go any deeper, please allow me the time to define the word *virgin*. To be virgin means to be morally beyond reproach; it means to be modest, pure, and uncorrupted; it means to be absolutely free from evil. Now we know that the Bible states we were all born *into sin*. Please pay close attention to this statement! Again, the Word of God says we were *born into sin*, not that we were sinners. We become sinners through our choices, but through choosing to abide and have a life in Jesus Christ, we become free from sin, which in return makes us servants of righteousness. Romans 6:1–4 states,

What shall we say [to all this]? Are we to remain in sin in order that God's grace [favor and mercy] may multiply and overflow? Certainly not! How can we who died to sin live in it any longer? Are you ignorant of the fact that all of us who have baptized into Christ Jesus were baptized into His death? We are buried therefore with him by the baptism into death so that just as Christ was raised from the dead by the glorious [power] of the Father, so we too might [habitually] live and *behave* in newness of Life. (AB, emphasis added)

Being morally beyond reproach, free from evil, and an uncorrupted person reflects your new life. Your past does not dictate how and when the favor falls. However, the state you are currently in when the favor falls does dictate the manifestation of your promise. So I ask you, what condition are you in right now? What is your heart like right now?

What is your spirit like right now? While you are expecting God's favor, can He find modesty, purity, and honesty in your heart? Because remember this: Esther's blessing has an assignment! God wants to bless you, and God wants to use you. His heart is to anoint you. God wants to make His name great through you. He is sending out an appeal! The King is looking for somebody that will obey Him.

Favor has been called a lot of things, but most favor is a direct result of your obedience to God. Are you ready to obey God? We can't get upset about what's happening for somebody else when all we have to do is obey God. Esther found favor because Vashti disobeyed a direct order. Just take a closer look at this: one woman's disobedience produced her own replacement, and another's woman's obedience produced placement. Are you a candidate for favor? Don't be discouraged about what has not happened yet in your life or spiritual walk; instead, take comfort in knowing that God is setting you up. Isaiah 41:18 states, "I will open rivers in high places and fountain in the midst of valleys: I will make the wilderness a pool of water and the dry land springs of water." This is the type of God we serve. He can take nothing and make it into something. He is the God of miracles! It may have seemed as if you have been in a dry season, a desert, or that you have been wandering the wilderness without purpose. You may have seen miracles happen for others or blessings fall upon everyone except you, but God is about to establish His principles in you. Favor is about to be revealed to you. That is the reason you've made it this far. He has put dreams inside of you, and He has given you the desire to touch the world with your gift or with the vision He's instilled in you. I am here to tell you that God has not forgotten you. Just when you feel you are left all alone, God has a divine assignment awaiting you.

An example of this can be found in Esther 2:5–7, which states, "Now in Shushan the palace there was a certain Jew, whose name was Mordecai, and he brought up Hadassah, that is Esther his uncle's daughter: for she had neither father or mother, and the maid was fair and beautiful whom Mordecai, when her father and mother were dead, took for his own daughter." Mordecai was Esther's divine connection, being an officer of the court, and Esther's guardian; he had inside information on the opening position of the queen. Mordecai was in the right place at the right time. Though Esther was orphaned by her parents, God had divinely connected her with someone to take her to the next level of favor.

Pay close attention to your divine connections, as these are the ones that God will use to help thrust you to your next level or assignment! Oh, somebody get happy here, because God is sending you help! Now pray this as often as you can: "Lord, I thank you for raising up somebody to use his or her ability and influence to be a blessing unto me!"

The Bible depicts Mordecai as a man of wisdom and goodness. Esther 2:11 states that Mordecai walked every day before the court to know how Esther did and what should become of her. For favor to flow freely, associate yourself with those who may impart wisdom into your life. Seek out those who are sincerely concerned about your future. People who will not intercede for you will try to hinder the flow of God's favor in your life. Bad associations will keep favor from finding you. He will give you the right sketch artist to draw the vision up for you, someone who won't distort, contort, or "misconstrue" the vision. Don't give up on your dream, and don't give up on your vision, for favor is trying to find you.

Some dreams may seem too big, or some may seem foolish to the natural eye, but favor allows and creates what you couldn't achieve on your own. Favor is not your responsibility to make happen. If God is telling you to do some foolish things, that means favor is trying to find you.

If it makes no sense to human beings, then know that favor is trying to find you.

About thirteen years ago, when I first got saved, I was in a relationship with a very nice young man. The Holy Spirit spoke to me about two weeks after giving my life to Christ and said "let him go." I knew we weren't equally yoked at the time; however, I had been praying, "Save him, God." After expressing to him my desire to totally surrender and live for God, his respect for me grew, and he proposed to me. *Praise God* is what my natural mind said. While he was placing the ring on my finger, I heard the Holy Spirit say again, "He is not your husband." Crying and distraught, I told the young man that I could not marry him. He truly didn't understand, but I had to obey the voice of the Lord. In releasing myself from the relationship, I did not realize that God was directing my path for His divine purpose for my life. It seemed foolish to the natural person inside me to let this good guy go, but through my obedience, favor was trying find me. It was not just about me, but this decision involved my destiny and the future that God preordained for me. At the time of the proposal, God had a saved, blessed young man praying for a wife. That man, my husband, was divinely placed in the church that I was strategically sent to.

He is now a pastor and my biggest supporter. God ordained this man to push me to new levels and to accomplish things I would have never thought to be possible for my life. He pushed me into my destiny. It may seem foolish to the natural human being inside you, but obey God. Now that's a divine connection. God wants to endow you and pour out upon you an abundance of spiritual blessings.

Favor needs someone who will stand out in a crowd, someone who won't fit in with everybody. It shouldn't displace you when someone doesn't like you. When you have favor, God will anoint someone to love you. Favor needs someone bold enough to say no to man and yes to God; it needs someone who walks in an unusual anointing that is not trying to be like everybody else. Favor desires someone who will believe God against the odds. Favor actually looks for people who are not necessarily qualified for certain things but are willing to be foolish enough to apply for them.

When favor is trying to fall, it doesn't matter where you come from or whose bloodline you come out of. Being raised in the church is not a prerequisite for favor and neither is being brought up in the streets. Favor does not care how much knowledge you have; nor does it seek to know where you live. God took an orphan girl, parentless (I believe she probably felt rejected, lonely and oppressed), and set her before great men. It only took one door to release her into a lifetime of blessings and opportunity.

I know for some of you reading this book, you've been waiting on your day to go before the King. You have been looking for your one door and waiting on your once-in-a-lifetime opportunity. I know things seem dim now, and some days are discouraging. Some of you may even feel orphaned and left alone. But for what God is getting ready to do, it's only going to take one door, one chance, one opportunity, one platform, and the one right ear to hear. The opening of this one door shall be the releasing of many blessings, God's divine favor.

God is releasing the Esther inside of you. He is decreeing an anointing of favor over your life today. It is the blessing that takes women higher, men higher, ministries higher, and families higher. Favor will take you from a past of obscurity to your name being known all over the land. It is the blessing of the motherless to become a mother of many nations. It is the blessing of the single woman to marry the most eligible bachelor in the land! Now that's favor! Esther and Mordecai walked into the presence of the king and received some of their enemies' possessions. The house of Haman is coming into your hands. Favor will bring back what you lost and give you more. Joel 2 states "And I will restore unto you what the locust has eaten". Now receive this decree and this endowment in Jesus' name. Favor! Favor! Favor! Favor! Grace and divine favor—an abundance of blessings and a spiritual endowment—have been released to give you favor with God and human beings.

I bind every spirit that resembles the house of Haman and everything that mocks or holds up the assignment of God on your life. We speak to the spirit of the oppressed, and as Psalm 72:4 says, we break it into pieces.

God, I thank You for favoring me and bringing me into my righteous possessions. Isaiah 45:1–3 states, "Open for me the gates of righteousness that I may receive the treasures of darkness and hidden riches in secret places." In this assignment, I will walk boldly and unapologetically because you have raised me up for such a time as this.

5

Chosen to Be Favored

And the Lord said "Arise, anoint him, for this is he!"

—1 Samuel 16:12

The Greek word for *anoint* is *mashach*, which means not only to anoint but also to smear or consecrate.

To be anointed is to be specially set apart for an office or function. Typically, this took place in the Old Testament with kings, as with David. He was picked out by God and set apart for a special task, anointed to reign as a king over Jerusalem. David was chosen to receive God's favor. He was the youngest of eight sons and the most common in position and stature.

Before David was anointed with the horn of oil, God selected him and granted him favor. The Bible states, "And the Lord said to Samuel, how long will thou morn for Saul, seeing I have rejected him from reigning over Israel? Fill thine horn with oil and go. I will send thee to Jesse the Bethel-mite, for I have provided me a King among his sons" (1 Samuel 16:1). While David tended the sheep and kept the flock, the favor of God abided on his life. Many of us are performing our everyday tasks and duties unaware that God has already chosen us to receive His anointing. The plans that the Lord has for us are so much bigger than the plans we often have for ourselves, and if we were to wait for validation from those who are around us, we would probably never walk in our divine destinies.

David is the perfect example of your average, everyday, ordinary young man who God looked upon and spoke "*ratsah,*" meaning, "for I am pleased with you." The Scriptures do not record whether Jesse knew that God had selected his son as king. As a matter of fact, 1 Samuel 16:10 reads that Jesse made all seven of his sons pass before Samuel, never even offering David entry into the ceremony. But Samuel requested that Jesse send for David. Isn't this like God to choose the one that all others wouldn't have expected? But that's what favor is; you don't have to look for it; it finds you. Never look for a human being to put you in the right positions, and never look for a human being to solve all your problems. Never allow yourself to feel as if you're stuck in a certain forum or arena, but always rely on the favor of God. Favor will bring you out of situations that seem impossible, circumstances that seem overwhelming, and arenas that appear to be dead ends. Favor is a gift from God; it will direct your entire future. It is a continuous flow of God's miracles. Favor is a failure-blocker and a divine door to success. The anointing prepares you to walk in God's favor.

The Bible states, "So David prevailed over the Philistine with a sling and with a stone and smote the philistine and slew him; but there was no sword in the hand of David" (1 Samuel 17:50). Was David already picked out to win this battle? Yes! Did the Philistines and Goliath judge David on his appearance? Yes! What they didn't know was that David had already been anointed. Somebody shout, "I am anointed!" Proverbs 8:35 states, "For who finds Me finds life and shall obtain favor from the Lord." To know God and have His spirit are the keys to walking in His favor with the manifestations of victory. The anointing gives you the ability to see the favor displayed in your life and the assurance that no obstacle, common or uncommon, will ever overtake you. David had confidence that God would show up for him, and with a slingshot and a stone he defeated the giant: "And David put his hand in his bag ..." (1 Samuel 17:49).

Sometimes there will be victory on one side and defeat on the other, and the only thing that separates you is the valley of decision. Israel represents your promise, your call, your mandate, and your breakthrough. The Philistines represent the flesh, the mountain, the dilemma, and your struggle. In the midst of all of this was David, and he represents God's favor. He made a decision that he could take the giant out. You can have what you say. Speaking the wrong things or negative utterances, however, can hinder the flow of God's favor. The Philistines had a history of intimidating people because of their height and size. In addition, because of the past victories, they were convinced they would win again. But despite all the intimidating factors, David boldly declared, "I will defeat this giant!" This is one of the key ways that favor is manifested in a believer's life—through faith-filled confessions. Proverbs 18:21 states, "Death and life are in the power of the tongue, and they that love it shall eat the fruit thereof." The next time you are faced with an issue that seems impossible, confess the favor of God. Speak it over your life, and watch common battles be turned to uncommon victories.

David put his hand in his bag and pulled out five smooth stones. The number five biblically represents God's grace. Grace means to show favorable acts of kindness or to be in favor with. David must have known something within himself to choose God's biblical number of favor to defeat the giant with. He had five stones, but it only took one. When God has anointed and chosen you, you will have an unlimited ability to prosper, succeed, and conquer everything that comes against you. Remember, when David put his hand (five fingers) in his bag and pulled out those five stones, grace was meeting up with grace. Zechariah 4:7 states, "Who art thou, O great mountain? Before Zerubbabel thou shalt become a plain and he shall bring for the head stone thereof with shouting, crying grace, grace unto it." David had this kind of experience, the grace; he had a grace blessing.

I can remember hearing a very prophetic message on a particular Scripture out of Zechariah. I'm not really able to quote now what I heard, but I have never forgotten those two very powerful words: "Grace, grace." Grace, to the believer, often is associated with mercy, so it seems so unobtainable. Now we must realize that grace is the same gift given by God to human beings, but it testifies to the ability of Christ. God extends His graciousness and His divine favor in His own sovereign way and will to whomever He chooses. After hearing this profound teaching on Zechariah 4:7 and realizing that the mountain represents human obstacles, I have come to understand that we sometimes have no human authority over trials, tribulations and unfortunate areas of struggle in our lives. (is that better?) those circumstances we sometimes have. But hearing such a revelatory message on confessing *grace, grace* to every obstacle that appears to be a mountain and then watching it be brought down to a plain (a mere molehill) has changed my life.

At the time I received this teaching, my husband was unemployed for two years due to a job layoff. Receiving word that a very popular company had openings in their microbiology lab, he went and applied. The company, Green Giant (owned by General Mills), received over seven hundred applicants for the one position! You know who the Jolly Green Giant is? Well, he is posted at the front of the company. My husband, our two children, and I would take a thirty-minute ride every day for almost one month and look at the Jolly Green Giant and say to it, "Grace, grace!" Well, need I say more? My husband was contacted and was offered the job. God took the mountain of unemployment and turned it into a molehill with our shouts of "Grace, grace!"

As Zechariah taught, with divine favor your circumstances can be changed. As the temple was rebuilt, so shall everything in your life, your family, or your ministry be rebuilt with God's divine favor. One minute of favor will allow you to receive what others have worked a lifetime for. Favor is better than riches and gold. This is what happened with David; grace changed his life. There will be a pivotal point, a one-time experience, that will release you into your destiny, so don't you miss it. It may appear to be an enemy, but the greatest enemy in your life may be that thing that pushes you into the favor of God. In 2 Corinthians 12:9, the Bible says, "And he said unto me; My *grace* is sufficient for you, for My strength is made perfect in weakness. Most gladly therefore, will I rather glory in my infirmities, that the power of Christ may rest upon me" (emphasis added).

God-promised favor is all you need when you are feeling weak or infirmed, depressed, lonely, rejected, or confused. To live in God's favor is to be covered and protected in every area of your life. Don't just associate favor with positions, possessions, or opened doors. When sickness or infirmity comes your way, or when it comes to someone you know, thank God for His favor, which includes His freely bestowed blessings, gifts, and acts of kindness. This is also His mercy. Divine favor will bring victory into every situation in your life. Favor with the anointing will bring you through. Romans 8:31 states, "If God be for us, who can be against us?" David prevailed! Favor will kill your Goliath; it will kill anything that defies your God.

6

Connected to Favor

And Ruth said, entreat me not to leave you, or to return from following after you. For wherever you go, I will go and wherever you live, I will live. Your people shall be my people and their God my God."

—Ruth 1:16

The manifestation of living in God's favor often is established through your divine connections. These connections include relationships, associations, or affiliations supernaturally brought together by God in a harmonious fashion. I like what the American Heritage College Thesaurus gives for the fifth definition of *connection*. It states that a connection is an acquaintance who is in a position to help a contact or source. Pray for divine connections. Divine connections are the ones that God will place in your life who are in a position to help your spiritual, natural, social, or economic state. There is always somebody that God has ordained for certain seasons of your life to be your contact or source. This was who Naomi was for Ruth, her contact and her source. Ruth did not go looking for Naomi, but God brought Naomi to Ruth. Diehl me was a contact to a life that Ruth never really knew. Though it appeared Naomi did not have much to actually give Ruth, her connection with them was more than natural, it was spiritual. There was something in Ruth that connected to Naomi's spirit, and she was not willing to let it go. Her husband was dead, and she had no child to keep her connected. But there was a deposit made to Ruth stating that she was dedicated to see the outcome of her divine connection. She was seeking something more than she ever had before. Matthew 6:33 states, "But seek ye first the kingdom of God and all of His righteousness and all these things shall be added unto you." Ruth had a desire to know who Naomi's God was. This released even greater favor in her life. This set up Ruth to receive all the things that were to be added to her life.

Many times people seek out divine connections, by which they mean ways to get in with the popular crowd or to be noticed by a specific individual. They network and even will drive certain cars to gain someone's attention they feel is important. In many cases, they may seek out things to make themselves seem important. But the Bible says that instead of seeking people, places, or things, we should "*seek the kingdom of God!*" Seek after the rules of God, the nature of God, and the laws of God, according to biblical principles (Exodus 20:1–17; Galatians 5:22). Ruth had a mind to seek the nature of God and to become associated with all of those who were in covenant with Him unselfishly. If favor is not always evident in your life, take an evaluation and see what you've been seeking, who you are connected to, and what your associations are.

Naomi became a source for Ruth, a way to leave a country only good for grazing flocks of sheep and goats, but not good enough to fulfill the destiny God had for her. Naomi's association became Ruth's association. Ruth became connected to her source. It's always good to be in the will of God, because even through adversity, God's favor will show up.

Ruth 1:1 states, "In the days when the judges ruled, there was a famine in the land. And a certain man of Bethlehem of Judah went to sojourn in the country of Moab, he, his wife and his two sons." Marriages between the Israelites and the Moabites were not forbidden; there was an exclusion, however, that no Moabite or any his or her descendents would enter the assembly of the Lord, even down to the tenth generation. Most theologians agree that the number ten would signify completion, which would mean as long as any person would live. But Ruth was clearly a distinct exception to the exclusion. Ruth's story reflected God's love for many through the evidence of His bringing a Moabite into His lineage. It doesn't matter who you are, or where you come from, when God wants to release His favor on your life, nothing can stop it. Though Naomi left Bethlehem because of unpleasurable circumstances, God was ordering her footsteps. After losing her husband and two sons, Naomi appeared to have nothing to offer her two daughters-in-laws, Ruth and Orphah. Naomi insisted they retreat back to the land of Judah and return home to her people. Ruth 1:15 says, "'Look,' said Naomi, 'your sister-in-law is going back to her people and her god's. Go back with her.'"

Yet, Naomi had a witness who divinely connected the two; although Ruth lost her husband, the divine connection still released her into the favor of God. Some people you may naturally not have anything in common with, but God has divinely connected you and your relationships to produce an abundance of blessings. Ruth, in 2:10–12, says "Why have I found favor in your eyes?" and Boaz answers, "I had been made fully aware of all you have done your mother-in-law since the death of your husband … The Lord recompenses you for what you have done and a full reward is given you by the Lord God of Israel, under whose wings you have come to take refuge" (AMP). Here is a shor summary of this chapter's lesson.

1. Divine Connection
2. Obedience
3. Will of God

Ruth's obedience caused her to stay in the will of God and recognize her divine connection.

In the course of writing this book, I became pregnant with my third child. It was an unplanned and rather surprising gift from God. Just one year prior, out of obedience, I closed my business that produced a very nice sum of income, and we began to struggle a little. My youngest child was five, and I thought I was finished having children, especially now that things had become a little tight. I asked the Lord why I had to become pregnant then, after had I closed the business. Why didn't this happen two years prior, when I could've afforded whatever I wanted? Little did I know that God was setting me up to demonstrate His uncommon favor. Because I hadn't really planned on having any more children, I had given everything away to others and to charities. In 1999, I gave birth to my first child, Elias James, and in the year 2000, I gave birth to another boy, Joel Demetrius Fambro. Well, of course, I was hoping for a girl, especially since I had already given birth to two sons and then gotten rid of all their baby clothes. I wasn't working, only ministering on occasion as the Lord would allow. So, I began to look at my circumstance, not really expressing to anyone how I felt, but internally conversing with God. I can remember, when I was about two months pregnant, that in intercessory prayer a prophetic word came concerning my unborn child. The prophetic word was, "God said this child was ordained by Him, and this was His doing; before the baby comes forth, he/she shall have everything needed." Now here's where *charitoo* comes in, which, again, means to cause to find favor. The very next day, I went to the store and ran into an old coworker who worked at the local hospital where I once was employed. She asked how I was doing, and I simply replied "great and pregnant" with a smile. Before I left the store, she said she wanted to bless me, and she came and found me. The favor of God was revealed, and I left with heaps of blessings for my unborn child. Not even twenty-four hours after the prophetic word was given, God displayed His favor in my life, and that was just the beginning. The favor of God surrounded me like a shield. It was my fence against any obstacles or dilemmas.

Sometimes, when it looks as though you have lost, or some things appear empty, God will send you overflow. I experienced the most breathtaking and lavish baby shower one could ask for. And before my child had arrived, he was more blessed than I could ever have imagined.

David Royal Fambro was born March 8, 2006, and has been living in abundance all the days of his life. From lack to abundance, because of divine connections, God continues to rain in his life daily. It doesn't matter what you think about a situation, when favor is released, it will bring glory back to God. I thought if I had a girl it would be more exciting because I previously had boys. But God shows David Royal Fambro to be a manifestation of His unlimited favor.

The favor of God is better than riches; he put me into a position, through my obedience, to experience the same favor as Ruth. Sometimes, God wants you to release yourself from what you know and what is comfortable for you in order for you to experience *more*! Favor always brings more into your life. The favor of God will bring to you what money cannot buy. I feel so blessed to have been a part of God's divine plan. Look how Ruth's life turned out all because of her obedience, her willingness to hear God, and her humility to stay divinely connected. She became one in the lineage of our Lord and Savior Jesus Christ. The favor of God will bring you spiritual and natural blessings.

Remember that divine connections are very important, because choosing the wrong connections could cause you to move in the wrong direction. Often choosing the right connections can propel you into your God-given destiny. Favor is very much equated with destiny. It's the sole purpose for God's releasing His blessings upon your life. The Bible says that a good person's steps are ordered of the Lord. When great destiny waits, the Enemy will often send someone in your path to hinder your walk. If you have any type of discomfort about someone who comes into your life, pray for discernment. It doesn't mean that when things go wrong, it's not the will of God. Look at Ruth: her husband died, and she could have thought this was the end of her relationship with Naomi, but she was connected to the right spirit. Try the spirit by the spirit, and see if it is of God. Some connections will produce the manifestation of the wrong spirit. The Bible encourages us to try the spirit, discern it, weigh it, and compare it to the will of God for your life. If it doesn't glorify God, if it doesn't produce spiritual blessings, and if it feeds your flesh, then you cannot go to the next level, and favor will not manifest for you; it's the wrong spirit. Remember how the Enemy works: he's a thief who comes to kill, steal, and destroy. He doesn't just try to destroy your salvation; the

Enemy also comes to invade your joy, your peace, your favor, and your divine destiny.

Stay connected! Stay connected to the source! Jesus says, "I am the way the truth and the life". Look for God-given qualities and for someone who will speak into your life. Naomi acted as a spiritual midwife to Ruth. Favor is inside of you, but sometimes you need divine connections to help birth the blessing and produce the manifestation of it. I've had the privilege to be placed or divinely connected to spiritual men and women of God who recognize the favor of God on my life and push me into my God-given destiny. There will often be moments in your life, precious moments and once-in-a-lifetime moments, that you don't want to miss. These are the moments you must seize and not let pass you by. Ask God to open your eyes that you might see into individuals' spirits and to open your ears that you might hear what He says concerning individuals who cross your path.

Take the Limits Off

What restrictions have you placed on your life or on God that will keep you locked in a box? Jabez said, "Enlarge my territory; keep evil away from me and let me prosper."

Just because you haven't seen it doesn't mean it cannot be done. I urge you today by the spirit of God to take the limits off. God wants to use you for His glory and to take every negative experience and work it for your good.

Growing up, I was the child nobody remembered (not in a negative way; I was just very shy). I felt I didn't have an important voice. But God had a purpose for my life, to speak into countless people's lives from day to day; this is a territory that I never thought I would walk in. I can truly say in my life that God will get the glory! To do the unexpected breaks traditions and barriers, and to excel in areas that others never thought you would reveals God working in your life. Favor is for everyone. God is not a respecter of persons. He wants to reveal Himself in supernatural, unusual ways. Expect a move from God, even as you read this. Look for his appearances day to day. I promise you, after reading this book you will see His hand and manifestations more than you ever have before.

7

Destined to
Be Favored

But for this purpose I have raised you up, to show you my power, so that my name may be proclaimed in all the earth.

ESV bible— Exodus 9:16

Favor is when destiny and sovereignty meet up so that the will and purpose and plan of God can be performed in your life. Moses had a destiny and was born under a sovereign God. There was a bigger plan that far outweighed the Enemy's plan. Whatever God has destined to rise up, it is the Enemy's desire to kill, but what a mighty God we serve! Did you know that the Devil knows who you are and is afraid of your very existence? Exodus 1:16 says, "And he said, when you do the office of a midwife to the Hebrew women, and see them upon the stools; if it be a son, then ye shall kill him." Like Jesus, the Devil thought he had him, but God made a way of escape. Moses also was sent to be a deliverer, an answered prayer for a lost generation, bound by the Enemy. The enemy understands that it only takes one person to change a situation or even a nation. That is why he doesn't want you to know you were *destined to be favored.*

Remember, Satan spent a whole lot of time with God and understands His mindset and knows God has a heart for His people. As long as you are willing to be used, God will favor your destiny, day after day, month after month, and year after year.

God wants His power to be demonstrated through His people so that His name may be glorified. Do you realize that every time the manifested power of God is displayed to you as a believer, that's favor? God's favor brings revelation to your life. The Word of God says, "I give you power to tread on serpents, scorpions … And over all the power of the enemy." This is why the Enemy is intimidated by you. When you know who you are in God, you will fill the Enemy with fear and frighten him into submission. There will be times when the Devil will not be able to touch you. Have you ever experienced this? You can tell that Satan's weapon has been formed, but you know it cannot prosper. At the name of Jesus, demons tremble. The Enemy literally shakes and quivers when another soul begins to operate within God's call. All of heaven will back you up and make a way for destiny to spring forth. As the Bible says, "By this, I know that thou favor me, because my enemy does not triumph over me" (Psalm 41:11).

What an experience! Have you ever experienced a victory over an enemy who had already predetermined your downfall? We praise God that He is pleased with you because your enemies didn't overtake you!

Stay connected to the source! There are five things that will hinder the favor of flow in your life:

1. Procrastination
2. Sin
3. Slothfulness
4. Disobedience
5. False Humility

When you stay connected to favor, God will reveal these areas of lack in your walk with Him. Procrastination, which is delayed obedience, is the same as being disobedient. It is a hindrance to your progress, a setback to your growth, and it binds up your blessings. Take the opportunity! Walk in God's favor boldly and allow Him to be displayed as evidence that you were created for purpose and destiny.

Sin has no place before God and will automatically disqualify you for advancement. Always be transparent and have your heart open before God so that sin can be revealed. Check your thoughts, your heart, and your actions. Evaluate your motives; weigh them against God's already established principles. If you find a snare, repent and walk in full deliverance; God still has a plan for your life. Slothfulness is a lot like procrastination. Being hesitant when God has giving a direct word to walk in causes decreased favor and delays God's promises for your life. Slothfulness can also be extreme laziness. Be careful of the spirit of laziness, for it seeks to blind you to time. Stealing time is a trick of the Enemy to distract you, make you lose focus, and get you to be blind to the urgency of the moment.

Disobedience is a direct violation of God's will and kingdom. As stated earlier, Saul lost the anointing to be king because of disobedience. It is always better to be obedient than to sacrifice the favor of God. Direct disobedience will not only bring you out of the will of God, but it will also bring disdain to your relationships with other people. It will bring lack on all levels, and it will label you as one who is not to be trusted. Favor seeks out obedient hearts. Always examine your heart, for out of it flows the issues of life.

Finally, we come to false humility. False humility is a walking lie. It is manifested through doubt, fear, insecurity, and lack of confidence. It distorts reality and suppresses the truth. The word of God is clear on this particular subject: false humility will cause you to miss out on your blessing; it is the flip side of pride. It's in Him (Christ) that we move and have our beings. The truth is that false humility is a cover-up for a heart that seeks attention but appears to be meek and submissive. God wants to pour out in your life. Allow Him to bless you sincerely. Do not discredit the favor of God because of egoism. Value His blessings as much as His Word, deliverance, and healing. Psalm 35:27 states, "Let them shout for joy, and be glad, that favor my righteous cause: yea, let them say continually, let the Lord be magnified, *which hath pleasure in the prosperity of His servants*" (emphasis added). God wants to bless and favor you.

I am praying for all of you, every person who reads this book and desires to walk in extreme favor. I am praying that your heart manifest the prosperity God intended. I'm praying that you gain an understanding of His will for your life. Just as the Lord spoke to Jehoshaphat in 2 Chronicles 20:20 and admonished the people that if they praised God, He would show up, today I speak prophetically into your life. You will begin to prosper in ways you never imagined. The arm of the Lord is about to be released in your life to a greater extent. There will be opportunities and doors that will open for you that will be unexplainable by human beings. I see, by the Spirit of God, people and business that have struggled for years. God is about to give you unmerited favor and release the funds you have been praying for. God is about to release your ideals and inventions to the right people at the right time. Get in position! I feel a recovery and restoration anointing; I hear the Lord saying that payback and back pay are coming! As the Lord said to David, you shall recover all. By the Spirit of God, you're about to walk away with the spoils. How ignorant and arrogant of the Enemy that he thought he could get away with your stuff. Your purpose was declared ahead of time, and from the day of conception your destiny was set into motion! Now I command you, ma'am, sir, boy or girl, rise up! Get into position! This is not just your time; it is God's time, and His favor is without limits.

Father, I pray Your people experience extraordinary, uncommon favor. Let them know and understand Your mysteries. Let all things hidden be made manifest, and reveal the things that belong to them. As 1 Corinthians 10:16

says, "Let them drink from the cup of blessing," and let it overflow.

Now is the time, the set time for God to show compassion on Zion; the time to favor Zion is now! Get ready, people of God: there is a fresh wind flowing your way. Amen!

Confessions of Favor

Here are Scriptures that I believe will help you with your daily walk in favor. Read them every day. Quote them as much as possible. Believe that God's hand will be seen in your season, and take all the limits off of God.

For Power

2 Samuel 5:20

"And David came to Baalperazim, and David smote them there, and said, the LORD hath broken forth upon mine enemies before me, as the breach of waters. Therefore he called the name of that place Baalperazim."

Job 22:28

"Thou shalt also decree a thing, and it shall be established unto thee; and light shall shine upon thy ways."

Mark 11:23

"For verily I say unto you, That whosoever shall say unto this mountain, Be thou removed, and be thou cast into the sea; and shall not doubt in his heart, but shall believe that those things which he saith shall come to pass; he shall have whatsoever he saith."

For Sickness

Psalm 91:10

"There shall no evil befall thee, neither shall any plague come nigh thy tent."

Isaiah 54:17

"No weapon that is formed against thee shall prosper; and every tongue that shall rise against thee in judgment thou shall condemn. This is the heritage of the servants of Jehovah, and their righteousness which is of me, saith Jehovah."

Psalm 118:17

"I shall not die, but live, and declare the works of the LORD."

Psalm 91:7

"A thousand may fall at your side, ten thousand at your right hand, but it will not come near you."

Isaiah 53:5

"But He was wounded for our transgressions, He was bruised for our iniquities: the chastisement of our peace was upon Him; and with his stripes we are healed."

For Favor

Numbers 6:24–26

"Jehovah blesses thee, and keeps thee: Jehovah make his face to shine upon thee, and be gracious unto thee: Jehovah lift up his countenance upon thee, and give thee peace."

Psalm 68:19

"Blessed be the Lord, who daily loadeth us with benefits, even the God of our salvation. Selah."

Psalm 44:3

"For they gat not the land in possession by their own sword, neither did their own arm save them; But thy right hand, and thine arm, and the light of thy countenance, because thou was favorable unto them."

Leviticus 26:9

"For I will be leaning toward you with favor and regard for you, rendering you fruitful, multiplying you, and establishing and ratifying My covenant with you."

Job 42:10

"And the LORD restored the fortunes of Job, when he prayed for his friends: also the LORD gave Job twice as much as he had before."

1 Samuel 2:8

"He raises the poor from the dust and lifts the needy from the ash heap; He seats them with princes and has them inherit a throne of honor. For the foundations of the earth are the LORD's; upon them He has set the world."

Favor Nuggets from Lisa

Lisa Fambro
MINISTRIES

- One wind of favor can shift your destiny to another whole dimension!
- When you do for others what they cannot do for themselves, you will never lack God's favor!
- Some things didn't work out for you because they were birthed prematurely. Don't be discouraged … God says this time they will *thrive*. His favor is on them!
- You will defy odds that are up against you and gain *favor* where you have been counted *out*!
- Expect favor from uncommon places.

- You will say, "The momentum has shifted in my favor. There is a progressive move taking place, and I'm gaining motion by these series of events!"
- Favor will shift an atmosphere from natural to supernatural, ordinary to extraordinary, and common to uncommon.
- Just because you're tending sheep in the pasture doesn't mean God can't see you. Remain faithful; the anointing will reveal who you are! I speak the favor of David, Esther, and Joseph into your life. God is going to bring you from obscurity and place you before great men and women.

Your Personal Journal

Take the time to write out your dreams and make plain your thoughts. Favor and destiny await your movement!

❧

_____

_____

_____

_____

_____

Lisa Royal Fambro

Rholanda "Lisa" Fambro is a leader, teacher, and motivational speaker who operates under a prophetic anointing and uses her God-given gifts to relay the Word of God into the hearts of people everywhere. Lisa is a gifted counselor and listener, and her passion is to encourage and motivate men and women of God into their destinies. Lisa believes that no matter where you come from and what kind of life you have lived, God can transform you and make you effective for His kingdom purpose. A business owner, entrepreneur, and former radio host, Lisa has decided to live life on purpose and apply biblical principles to achieve God's plan for everyday living. A native of Camden, New Jersey, she now resides in Rockford, Illinois, where she ministers alongside her husband, Pastor James Fambro, at Christian Growth Center Church. She is the mother of three blessed seeds, Elias, Joel, and David.

Without a doubt, Lisa has a message for the masses; with a prophetic and profound word, she will challenge you to go beyond limited thinking and believe God for His unlimited favor in your life. Lisa desires to lead people to dream bigger, push past impossibilities, and live the life God intended.

To have Lisa Royal Fambro minister at your event or to order teaching CDs and other ministry products, please send a letter of interest to Lisa at the following address:

Lisa Royal Fambro
PO Box 8731
Rockford, IL 61126

To order books as teaching material for classes, women's groups, or events, please contact

Lisa Fambro Ministries via phone or e-mail:

815-873-1120
Lisafambro1@gmail.com

Printed in the United States
By Bookmasters